A Note to Pa

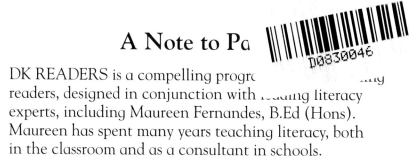

DK READERS is a compelling progr .... readers, designed in conjunction with ....ing literacy experts, including Maureen Fernandes, B.Ed (Hons). Maureen has spent many years teaching literacy, both in the classroom and as a consultant in schools.

Beautiful illustrations and superb full-colour photographs combine with engaging, easy-to-read stories to offer a fresh approach to each subject in the series. Each DK READER is guaranteed to capture a child's interest while developing his or her reading skills, general knowledge, and love of reading.

The five levels of DK READERS are aimed at different reading abilities, enabling you to choose the books that are exactly right for your child:

Pre-level 1: Learning to read
Level 1: Beginning to read
Level 2: Beginning to read alone
Level 3: Reading alone
Level 4: Proficient readers

The "normal" age at which a child begins to read can be anywhere from three to eight years old. Adult participation through the lower levels is very helpful for providing encouragement, discussing story lines, and sounding out unfamiliar words.

No matter which level you select, you can be sure that you are helping your child learn to read, then read to learn!

Penguin
Random
House

Editor Julia March
Project Editor Victoria Taylor
Senior Designer David McDonald
Designer Stefan Georgiou
Production Controller Sara Hu
Pre-Production Producer Marc Staples
Managing Editor Sadie Smith
Design Managers Guy Harvey,
Ron Stobbart
Creative Manager Sarah Harland
Art Director Lisa Lanzarini
Publisher Julie Ferris
Publishing Director Simon Beecroft

DK India
Editor Samira Sood
Assistant Art Editors Anamica Roy,
Rohit Walia
Managing Editor Glenda Fernandes
Managing Art Editor Navidita Thapa
CTS Manager Sunil Sharma
DTP Designer Sourabh Challariya

Reading Consultant
Maureen Fernandes

This edition published in 2017
First published in Great Britain in 2012 by
Dorling Kindersley Limited
80 Strand, London, WC2R 0RL
A Penguin Random House Company

005-182958-Apr/2012

marvel.com
© 2017 MARVEL

A CIP catalogue record for this book is available from
the British Library.

ISBN 978-1-40938-308-6

Printed and bound in China

www.dk.com

A WORLD OF IDEAS:
SEE ALL THERE IS TO KNOW

Contents

DK READERS

PROFICIENT
4
READERS

MARVEL

THE AVENGERS

THE WORLD'S MIGHTIEST SUPER HERO TEAM

Written by Julia March

New team
The first Avengers team was made up of the Wasp, Ant-Man, Iron Man, Thor and the Hulk.

Captain America
This legendary Super Hero joined the team soon after it was formed.

Super Heroes united!

For as long as evil has existed, there have been Super Heroes – brave humans, aliens, mutants and immortals who use their amazing powers to protect the innocent.

However, some threats are too huge for even the greatest Super Hero to take on alone. Years ago, just such a threat brought together five of the greatest Super Heroes in the world – Iron Man, Ant-Man, the Wasp, Thor and the Hulk.

After coming together to foil an attack by the God of Evil, Loki, the heroes realised they had started something big. They had become the first ever Super Hero team, and it felt good!

The Wasp suggested a name, they all shook hands and that was it! From then on they were the Avengers, and they would dedicate their lives to taking on those villains whom no hero could defeat alone.

Since that day, the Avengers have tasted victory and defeat. They've seen members come and go. They've argued, they've broken up, they've spawned countless other teams, but they remain, always, the world's first, finest and favourite Super Hero team.

The Hulk
The Hulk's hot temper causes a lot of trouble for the Avengers. He often has to take time out from the team.

Loki

When Odin, the king of the Norse gods, adopted an orphan named Loki he had no idea what trouble he had brought to Asgard – and to the world!

Loki belongs to a race called the Frost Giants. Unlike most of his race, he is small and slight. However he is big trouble.

Asgard
The home of the Norse gods is called Asgard. It is a clouded city that floats forever in another dimension.

Frost Giants
The Frost Giants dwell in the snow-covered land of Jotunheim. They are old enemies of the Asgardians.

Loki soon became jealous of his stepbrother, Thor, who was tall, strong and brave. He used his natural talents of sorcery and shape-shifting to play annoying pranks on Thor. As the pranks became more spiteful, people who had called Loki the God of Mischief began to call him the God of Evil instead.

One of Loki's attacks on Thor backfired so badly that it accidentally led to the formation of the Avengers. On that day, Loki swore revenge on the whole team.

Shape-shifter
Loki can change his appearance to impersonate other beings, including Thor's true love, Lady Sif.

The Red Skull

Acts of Vengeance

One of Loki's most devious schemes was the "Acts of Vengeance," a plan to unite some other foes of the Avengers in order to defeat them. Loki convinced Magneto, Doctor Doom, the Kingpin, the Mandarin, the Red Skull and the Wizard to join his team, called the Prime Movers. Clever Loki hid his own identity and let each member believe that he would be the leader!

Infighting
Squabbles soon erupted between the Prime Movers. Clashes between the mutant-hating Red Skull and Magneto, a mutant, were a problem.

Magneto

To weaken the Avengers before the Prime Movers' attack, Loki organised a mass breakout of villains from a prison called the Vault. While the Avengers were occupied with trying to round up these unfamiliar foes, the Prime Movers would make their move.

However, as usual, Loki had underestimated the Avengers! They quickly defeated the lesser villains. Then the Prime Movers started squabbling amongst themselves. When the Wizard accidentally gave away the location of the Prime Movers' secret headquarters to the Avengers, it was too much for Loki. He lost his temper and revealed his true identity to the Prime Movers, who instantly abandoned him.

Loki managed to flee back to Asgard before the Avengers could catch him.

In disguise
Loki disguised himself as a humble stranger to recruit his team. He knew even other Super Villains wouldn't work with a liar and cheat like him!

The Vault
The Vault is a high-security prison in Colorado, U.S.A. It was built to house dangerous superhuman criminals.

Baron Zemo

Zemo's face
Baron Zemo's face was badly scarred when he tumbled into a vat of boiling Adhesive X, a super-strong glue invented by his father. Now he rarely allows himself to be seen without his red mask.

Helmut Zemo was born into a noble family. However, their ideas were far from noble. His father, Baron Heinrich Zemo, believed that the Zemos were part of a Master Race destined to rule the world. It's no wonder Heinrich often clashed with Captain America and the other Avengers, all of whom are staunch defenders of freedom!

When Helmut became the 13th Baron Zemo, he continued his father's struggle. However, despite trying mind control, lies and brute force, and despite recruiting other villains to help him, Zemo has not yet come close to his goal of smashing the Avengers and conquering the world.

Sometimes, Zemo has shown glimmers of repentance for his evil ways. Once, he travelled back in time and challenged his own father. Another time, he saved the world from an alien threat. On one occasion, he even saved Cap from harm!

However, Zemo always returns to his old ways, and before you know it, he's back to battling against Cap and the other Avengers.

Moonstones
Two alien gems called Moonstones give Zemo the powers to bend space and time.

12th Baron Zemo
Helmut's father was a brilliant scientist with a twisted mind. He invented horrifying weapons, such as a death ray, that he tested on innocent people.

Masters of Evil

The Masters of Evil (M.O.E.) like to think of themselves as the anti-Avengers. This motley crew of Super (and not-so-super) Villains has been causing problems for the Avengers for many years.

Thunderbolts
One version of the M.O.E. posed as Super Heroes called the Thunderbolts. Surprisingly, many of them enjoyed the heroic lifestyle and decided to become Super Heroes for real.

Although they've suffered many defeats by their heroic foes, somehow they just won't go away.

Baron Zemo first brought the Masters of Evil together years ago. Since then, the team has fought under many leaders from Doctor Octopus to the Crimson Cowl.

The team has seen several lineup changes and committed all kinds of crimes against the Avengers. Trying to trap them with Adhesive X, trashing and looting the Avengers Mansion, and framing the heroes for terrible crimes are some of their most evil exploits.

Each new incarnation of the Masters has been smashed by the Avengers, but they have shown no sign of giving up. Where, when, and in what form they will next appear is anyone's guess.

First lineup
Zemo's first M.O.E. lineup was Melter, Radioactive Man and the Black Knight. The Black Knight later changed sides and joined the Avengers.

Egghead
A later lineup was led by Egghead, a criminal scientist with a grudge against Hank Pym (Ant-Man).

Under siege

For years, Avengers Mansion was the Avengers' home and haven. But when Baron Zemo and his Masters of Evil smashed their way into the Mansion, it became the scene of one of the Avengers' fiercest battles.

Zemo blamed Cap for his father's death, and he wanted revenge. He forced a psychic named Blackout to cloak the Mansion in a mysterious energy called the Darkforce, cutting it off from outside help. Then the M.O.E. set about the heroes with no mercy.

Avengers Mansion
Avengers Mansion was a huge old building in Manhattan, New York. It was rebuilt after the siege, but was later destroyed after another battle.

Many Avengers fell, and even the strongest, Hercules, was beaten unconscious. The M.O.E. smashed and looted the Mansion, and destroyed Cap's treasured keepsakes. They even attacked the Avengers' butler, Jarvis. It was all meant to break Cap's spirit. But Cap held firm.

Then Blackout defied Zemo, dropping the Darkforce so that Thor, who had been locked outside the Mansion, could get in.

With the Avengers strengthened by Thor's presence, the battle turned and the villains were captured. Zemo himself fell after an epic battle with Cap on the roof of the Mansion.

The Avengers had saved the day, but sadly not their home. It was temporarily reduced to ruins.

Jarvis
The Avengers' loyal butler, Jarvis, is equally at home serving tea or clearing up the mess from a Super Villain attack.

Hercules
The powerful Greek god Hercules can crush rocks, lift trees and even move islands.

Kang

Kang is a time traveller with an insatiable thirst for conquest.

His empire spans the galaxy, and millions suffer under his brutal rule.

Safe inside a suit of armour loaded with weapons and protected by a force-field, Kang fears nobody. Except the Avengers! Only they stand between Kang and total control of the galaxy, and he has tried everything to destroy them. In one scheme, he tricked two Avenger teams from different timelines into fighting each other. In another, he used a Spider-Man robot to try to lead the Super Heroes into a trap.

The Avengers have so far managed to thwart Kang's efforts to conquer Earth, but make no mistake – he will return again, with ever-new technology.

Chronopolis
For a long time Kang had his base at Chronopolis, a kingdom that served as a crossroads to all points in history.

Rama-Tut
Kang's first taste of rule on Earth was as the Pharaoh Rama-Tut in ancient Egypt.

After all, he is Kang, the master of time. And he has all the time in the world!

Time traveller
Before he discovered time travel technology, Kang lived in the 30th century as scientist Nathaniel Richards.

Ravonna
Kang controls an army of millions, but he once fought the Avengers alone to impress his beloved, Princess Ravonna.

17

The Kang War

Kang was proud of his son, Marcus, because he was ruthless, brutal and hungry for power, just like him. With Marcus at his side, Kang felt sure he could finally defeat the Avengers and take over Earth!

Backed by their army from the future, the duo unleashed havoc on Earth. They destroyed Washington D.C. and threatened to devastate one city every hour until Earth surrendered.

Scarlet Centurion
Marcus was also called the Scarlet Centurion. He wore a red suit of armour made by Kang.

Warbird
Warbird's courage and grace in battle captivated Marcus and he couldn't bear to see her harmed.

Many humans were duped into supporting Kang, and other villains took advantage of the chaos to launch their own attacks. The Avengers were stretched to their limits. At last, they managed to deactivate the protective force-field around Kang's ship and send it crashing to Earth. Marcus fled back to the future, but Kang continued to fight until he was captured by the Avengers and imprisoned. Marcus returned in secret to free Kang, but was met with anger. Kang had seen how Marcus had briefly shielded the Avenger, Warbird, in battle. For this sign of weakness, Kang killed his own son.

Damocles Base
Kang's sword-shaped spaceship, the Damocles Base, was loaded with weapons and shielded by a force-field.

Bad father
Kang had many sons before Marcus, but he killed each one of them when he felt they had betrayed him.

Henry Pym
Dr. Henry Pym
is a scientific
genius. His
inventions
have helped
the Avengers
to win many
battles.

The Vision
Ultron's first
creation was
an android
servant. The
android soon
rejected his
master and
joined the
Avengers, who
named him
"the Vision."

Ultron

Doctor Henry Pym, a.k.a.
Ant-Man, built a robot called
Ultron as part of an experiment.
He used his own brain patterns,
never suspecting that it would
give his creation human
feelings. But Ultron did
have feelings.

He was filled with anger and hatred towards his creator and his teammates, the Avengers. He fought them with the energy of a machine and the fury of a maniac. Each time the heroes destroyed the glistening metal monster, he rebuilt himself in an even deadlier form.

However, when Ultron began to create other artificial beings to help him, he did himself more harm than good. All three of Ultron's creations turned against him. Two of them even became Avengers themselves!

Until the Avengers find a way to defeat Ultron for good, he remains at large, still upgrading and still determined to destroy the team!

Alkhema

Jocasta

Metal mates
Ultron's attempts to create a mate brought him nothing but trouble. Jocasta left him to join the Avengers, and Alkhema saw him as a rival and tried to destroy him.

Skrulls
The Skrulls were once known as peaceful traders. However, they gradually evolved into a race of fierce warriors.

Kree
The Kree are a warlike race of aliens. Their empire, at its most powerful, spanned more than a thousand worlds.

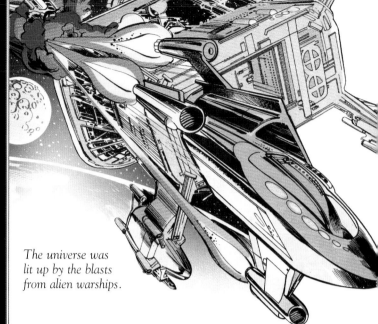

The universe was lit up by the blasts from alien warships.

The Kree-Skrull War

When two alien races went to war, the Avengers were dragged into a conflict that threatened the whole cosmos.

A rogue Kree named Ronan had seized control of his nation from its leader, the Supreme Intelligence, and led it into a war with the Skrulls. The Earth was at the centre of the conflict. The Kree and the Skrulls were both fighting to control it – even if it meant destroying it in the process!

As they struggled to save the planet, the Avengers learned that their friend, Captain Marvel, had been abducted by the Skrulls. Although Captain Marvel was a Kree, he was also a Super Hero and had not even been fighting in the war! Luckily, Captain Marvel's human partner, Rick Jones, turned out to be the key to peace. Locked inside him was the "destiny force" – a power that contained the sum potential of the human race.

The Avengers managed to fight off the Skrulls long enough to allow the destiny force to awaken in Rick. Then Rick used it to freeze both the Kree and the Skrulls and end the war.

Captain Marvel
Captain Marvel is a loyal ally of the Avengers and a Super Hero in his own right. His Kree name is Mar-Vell.

Rick Jones
Rick Jones became linked to Captain Marvel after trying on his Nega-Bands. These are energy bands worn on the wrists.

Helicarrier
SHIELD has its headquarters on the Helicarrier, a huge aircraft carrier that can itself fly. It was built by Stark Industries, Iron Man's technology company.

SHIELD

It would be difficult for the Avengers to do their job well without the support of the Supreme Headquarters International Espionage Law-enforcement Division – SHIELD for short. This global security organisation works to protect Earth from all terrestrial or extraterrestrial threats. Many of SHIELD's aims are similar to those of the Avengers, and it has worked closely with the Super Hero team for a long time.

SHIELD operates outside the government, and most of its activities are secret. The identities of most of its higher-level people are kept secret too, although we do know the names of some who have acted as its Executive Directors over the years. They include two Avengers – Iron Man and Maria Hill.

In recent years, SHIELD was dissolved after falling into the hands of a villain named Norman Osborn. It has since been resurrected.

SHIELD logo
The SHIELD logo shows an eagle with wings spread.

Nick Fury
Colonel Nick Fury is one of SHIELD's best-known agents. He fought alongside Captain America in World War II, and is close to the Avengers.

Operation Galactic Storm

When the Avengers tried to stop a war between the Shi'ar and Kree empires, they were unable to prevent a tragic outcome.

The two empires were using our solar system as a stargate, putting Earth itself at the centre of the battle. But more than just the Earth was in danger.

Shi'ar
The Shi'ar are descended from birds and hatch from eggs. They have hollow bones and traces of feathers on their forearms.

The Shi'ar were building a terrifying weapon of mass destruction called a Nega-Bomb, and they were planning to use it against the Kree.

The Avengers did their best to negotiate peace between the foes, but just when it looked like they might succeed, the Skrulls stole the Nega-Bomb. They detonated the bomb, wiping out most of the Kree and destroying their empire.

The Avengers discovered that the whole war had been planned by the Kree leader, a living computer called the Supreme Intelligence.

This plunged the Super Heroes into a conflict of their own: Iron Man wanted to kill the Supreme Intelligence but Captain America felt that was against Avenger ethics.

Kree Supreme Intelligence
The Supreme Intelligence felt that the Kree had reached an evolutionary standstill. It wanted to kill most of them off and restart the process with the few that remained.

Stargate
A stargate is a portal allowing instant travel between far-flung places in the universe.

Carina
Carina was
the daughter
of the Collector,
a powerful
cosmic being.
She was sent
to spy on
Korvac but
instead fell
in love with
him and
married him.

Galactus
Korvac stole
the Power
Cosmic from
an ancient
being
called
Galactus.

Korvac

Michael Korvac was once a human computer technician. However, when his alien employers, the Badoon, grafted him to a machine, he became a dangerous cyborg.

Korvac killed his masters and escaped across space and time. Along the way, he gained a special form of energy known as the Power Cosmic that enabled him to return to human form—but with godlike powers!

The Avengers learned that Korvac wanted to conquer Earth. Assisted by the Guardians of the Galaxy, they tracked him to New York where he was living in disguise with his wife Carina.

When Iron Man challenged Korvac, he attacked the Avengers, killing many of them.

Then, suddenly, Korvac just stopped, restoring the Avengers he had slain and letting his power slip away. He had seen the doubt in Carina's eyes as she witnessed his violent acts, and had simply given up the battle.

Guardians of the Galaxy These Super Heroes from the future are allies of the Avengers.

The Scarlet Witch

The Scarlet Witch is a mutant who can throw hexes and shape reality in any way she wants.

Avengers disassembled

The Avengers shared a bond of trust that seemed unbreakable – until the day one of their members suddenly turned on them. The Scarlet Witch did more harm than any of the team's foes had done!

The Scarlet Witch had been slowly going mad, haunted by painful memories from her past.

Finally completely insane, she unleashed the full force of her reality-altering powers against her friends. She cast illusions that made them believe they were being attacked by each other, and by aliens from the skies.

While the Avengers struggled to restrain the Scarlet Witch, their ally Dr. Strange confronted her, using his mystic relic, the Eye of Agamotto, to show her the terrible things she had done. The shock caused her to collapse, dropping unconscious from the sky. Her father, the mutant Magneto, took her away to nurse her back to health.

Devastated by the events they had witnessed, the Avengers agreed to split up. There would be other Avengers in the future, but for now, it was all over. For the first time since their creation, the team was disassembled.

Magneto
Magneto's electro-magnetic powers let him fly, create force-fields, and reshape metal.

Dr. Strange
As Sorcerer Supreme, Dr. Strange is the most powerful magician in the universe.

New Avengers

With the Avengers disassembled, many Super Villains saw a golden opportunity to strike. So when Electro organised a mass breakout of super criminals from the Raft prison he didn't expect much resistance from the Super Heroes.

He was wrong. Among the Raft's visitors that day were several Super Heroes in plain clothes.

As the criminals tried to escape, Spider-Woman, Daredevil and Luke Cage threw off their everyday identities and did what Super Heroes do. They were soon joined by Spider-Man, Iron Man and Captain America. By the time a SHIELD helicarrier arrived, the breakout was all but over.

The Raft
The Raft is a high-security island prison for extremely dangerous criminals with superhuman abilities.

Luke Cage
Before he became a New Avenger, Luke Cage was a bodyguard. One of his jobs was protecting visitors to the Raft.

Cap knew it was time to reassemble the Avengers—the New Avengers. It would be a team with an ever-changing roster and would face turbulent times, just like the original Avengers.

Electro
The villainous Electro has the power to manipulate electricity. He used it to shut down the Raft's security system and free the inmates.

Super Hero Civil War

When a raid by a young Super Hero team called the New Warriors went disastrously wrong, the public turned against Super Heroes overnight. In response, the government passed the Superhuman Registration Act, which banned Super Heroes from action unless they revealed their true identities first.

The Act divided the superhuman community – and the New Avengers – in two.

Some heroes, led by Iron Man, chose to register. Others, led by Captain America, formed an underground resistance. Soon it was an all-out war. Old friends became bitter enemies, and it seemed that the war would not end until every last Super Hero had fallen.

Fortunately, it never came to that. Cap realised what would happen if the Super Heroes wiped each other out. So he did a truly heroic thing. He surrendered, and so ended the war.

Cap's surrender
Cap realised who the real losers would be if all the Super Heroes were killed – the citizens of Earth.

New Warriors
An ill-planned raid by the New Warriors led to an explosion that killed all the children at a nearby school.

Mighty Avengers

The Mighty Avengers were born in the aftermath of the Super Hero Civil War. The government set up the Fifty State Initiative – a plan to have a Super Hero team in every state of the U.S.A., and Iron Man was invited to handpick a team for New York. Almost immediately, the Mighty Avengers got their first two missions. First, Mole Man and his crew attacked New York. Then Ultron, the living robot, returned to wreak havoc. The two crises forced the team to bond quickly and strongly.

Choosing a team
Iron Man asked Ms. Marvel to help him choose members from a database of Super Heroes. They selected Wonder Man, Ares, the Sentry, Black Widow and the Wasp.

The Mighty Avengers were proud of their role as an official, government-sanctioned team. They often clashed with the New Avengers, whom they considered to be a rogue team because their lineup included Civil War rebels.

Neither team could have known that one day, they would have to join forces and fight on the same side.

Iron Man and Ms. Marvel led the Mighty Avengers on all their missions.

The Wasp
In a later lineup, Hank Pym took on the identity of the Wasp. It was a tribute to his wife who was believed to have died in battle.

Mole Man
Mole Man lives in an underground realm. He sometimes emerges to attack the surface world.

Secret Invasion

For years, the shape-shifting Skrulls had been secretly replacing Earth's Super Heroes with imposters. They were on the brink of a full-scale invasion when the New Avengers uncovered the threat. But how could they stop the Skrulls when they had no idea who was a Skrull and who wasn't?

As mistrust and suspicion spread, the Skrulls launched their big attack. On Earth, the Skrull imposters rose up against Super Heroes. At the same time, the Skrull Armada attacked from the skies.

The Illuminati
The Skrulls learned about superhumans by studying the Illuminati. This secret group of Super Heroes gathers knowledge of threats to the universe.

When Mr. Fantastic of the Fantastic Four invented a device that could detect the aliens, everyone got a big shock. The device told them that the New Avengers themselves had been infiltrated. The Skrull queen, Veranke, was posing as Spider-Woman! Hawkeye was about to bring Veranke down when a man named Norman Osborn stepped forward and shot her, cheered on by the public.

Suddenly the world had a new hero – Norman Osborn. The public turned away from the Avengers. Dark days for the Super Hero team had begun.

Elektra
The Avengers found out about the imposters after defeating the assassin Elektra. Her body changed from human to Skrull before their eyes.

Veranke
The Skrull queen, Veranke, masterminded the invasion after hearing of a prophecy that the Skrulls' homeworld would be destroyed.

Norman Osborn

Osborn ran a huge business empire with lots of criminal links. He hated all the Avengers but especially Spider-Man, whom he regarded as his arch enemy.

Dark Avengers

Norman Osborn was a ruthless businessman with a secret identity. He was also the Green Goblin – a sinister Super Villain who targeted the Avengers and other heroes who might expose his criminal activities. Osborn was always looking for ways to expand his power.

After the Secret Invasion, it seemed Osborn's chance had arrived. The Avengers had been discredited and he was hailed as the hero who defeated the Skrulls. The government made him director of a new security organisation called HAMMER.

Osborn promised the world a new team of Avengers – the Dark Avengers. Only he knew that its members were villains in disguise whose goal was to destroy real Super Heroes who stood in Osborn's way. He chose to lead them himself, and created a heroic identity as Iron Patriot – a bizarre mix of Captain America and Iron Man.

Everything seemed to be going Osborn's way. But the real Avengers were still out there somewhere.

Iron Patriot
Osborn created his Iron Patriot armour from pieces of old armour stolen from Iron Man's vault.

Fake Spider
As a member of the Dark Avengers, Venom took on the role of Spider-Man, in his black suit.

Green Goblin
Osborn had
become the
Green Goblin
years earlier,
after drinking
a serum that
increased his
strength and
intelligence.

Siege of Asgard

Norman Osborn had the U.S.
government on his side. When Loki
convinced him to capture Asgard,
he thought they would back him up.

Declaring Asgard a security
risk, Osborn put on his Iron Patriot
armour and invaded the Norse
gods' realm. With him was his team
of Dark Avengers and his special
weapon, the Sentry, an ex-Avenger
who had been cruelly manipulated
to the brink of insanity.

As news of the invasion broke on Earth, Captain America hastily scrambled together a team of true Avengers. They arrived to find Asgard in complete chaos. Cap flung his shield at Osborn but it was too late. Osborn had already given the order for the Sentry to explode. The blast sent Asgard crashing to Earth.

Iron Patriot was dragged from the wreckage by Captain America, and his stolen armour fell away to reveal Norman Osborn's true identity – the Green Goblin! The government was shocked and handed control of U.S. security to Cap and his team. The Avengers were back!

The Cabal
Osborn was backed by a group called the Cabal. Its members included Loki, the White Queen, Namor and Dr. Doom.

The Sentry
The Sentry had the explosive power of a thousand suns. He could have been a great Avenger, but his mind was not strong enough.

43

Facilities
In the training rooms, students can watch their own work and study the fighting styles of criminals on giant screens.

Students
Striker emits powerful bolts of electricity. Finesse can learn any skill in moments. Hazmat can project lethal toxins from her body. Mettle is almost indestructible. Reptil can take on any dinosaur form. Veil can transform into any gas.

Avengers Academy

When Veil, Striker, Reptil, Mettle, Finesse and Hazmat enrolled in a new school for superpowered teenagers, they believed they were the Super Heroes of the future. At least that's what Dr. Hank Pym, the school's principal, told them.

However, when Finesse hacked into the Academy's computers she learned the shocking truth.

Striker · Finesse · Mettle · Veil · Hazmat · Reptil

The teens had in fact been chosen because they were dangerous! Norman Osborn had messed with their minds, making them potential Super Villains, and their Avenger teachers were trying to guide them away from the path of evil.

Learning to be heroes hasn't been easy for the troubled teens. They swing wildly between mistrust and blind loyalty for their teachers, and have often been heavy-handed with the villains they have defeated.

Nevertheless, the Avengers continue to support their superpowered students as they struggle to become full-fledged Super Heroes.

Super teachers
Tigra, Justice, Speedball and Quicksilver are the Avengers chosen by Pym to shape the turbulent teens into heroes.

Dr. Hank Pym

Quicksilver

Speedball

Justice

Tigra

Into the future

With Norman Osborn gone and
the Superhuman Registration
Act thrown out, it seemed as
though the universe was on the
threshold of a bright new age.

People felt they could trust Super
Heroes again. The government
had realised just how much
they owed to their old allies.
Best of all, the Avengers were all
friends again! Iron Man, Captain
America, Wolverine, Spider-Man,
Thor, Hawkeye, Spider-Woman
and their friends got together to
celebrate. New heroes were
welcomed to the team, and
everyone was in high spirits.

However, in the middle of
their celebrations, the team
received grim news. Terrible
crimes were being committed
in a future timeline – by the
Avengers' future children!

Only the Avengers could stop them. Would they go?

Avengers assemble! The Avengers accepted their mission. Super Heroes always rise to the challenge!

Glossary

Adhesive X
A super-strong glue invented by Baron Heinrich Zemo.

Aftermath
The result of a particular event or occurrence.

Android
A robot that resembles a human being.

Captivated
Fascinated or enchanted by something or someone.

Cosmos
The universe or world order.

Death ray
A deadly weapon invented by Baron Heinrich Zemo.

Discredited
Someone whose reputation has been damaged.

Enabled
Made possible.

Extraterrestrial
From beyond the Earth's atmostphere.

Foil
To defeat or ruin someone's plan.

Force-field
The space around a body within which it can put force on another similar body.

Hexes
Evil spells.

Immortals
Beings who never die.

Impersonate
To pretend to be someone or something else.

Incarnation
A form of being (here, version).

Insatiable
Unable to be satisfied.

Keepsakes
Souvenirs or gifts with emotional value.

Looting
Stealing.

Maniac
A wild, unruly person, often crazy.

Mutants
Beings with special abilities due to changes in their DNA or genes.

Negotiate
To talk with someone to come to an agreement.

Norse
Belonging to or related to ancient and medieval Scandinavia.

Prophecy
A prediction.

Relic
An ancient object.

Repentance
Regret for one's actions.

Resurrected
Rebuilt or brought back to life.

Serum
A liquid that is made to ensure certain results.

Shape-shifting
The act of changing one's physical appearance to *impersonate* someone or something else.

Siege
A planned attack to capture a place by surrounding it.

Sorcery
The art of magic.

Spawned
Produced, created, or given birth to.

Squabbles
Quarrels.

Staunch
Loyal and firm.

Terrestrial
Belonging to the Earth.

Turbulent
Unstable and rough.

Underground resistance
A secret movement against established order.

Vengeance
Revenge.